Words In The

by

Best Wishes

Chris Matthews *Chris.*

Illustrations by Reuben Curteis

1

Love to Sita Marie xxx Christine 2016.

First Edition: WORDS IN THE KEY OF LIFE

First published in Great Britain in 2016 by:
Chris Matthews

Designed and type-set in Times New Roman by Chris Matthews.

Cover design and colour illustrations by Reuben Curteis.

Printed and bound in Great Britain by Biddles Books.

Author Profile

I am originally from Wrexham N. Wales and began writing during my last years in school when I was encouraged to put my thoughts down on paper by an English teacher, Mr. Lee.

Writing gives the freedom to explore the mind's eye view of the world and to have a voice that can speak the things that would have remained unshared.

I have met some great people through writing at the various performance and share nights in Rotherham and always have time to listen to others; as it is through listening and observing others in life that I have drawn the most input for my own work.

A friend told me once, "There are only two rules here. First rule is there are no rules...Second rule...refer to rule one!".

In life "Those that mind don't matter....those that matter just don't mind!"

I hope you enjoy reading my work and that it encourages YOU to write for yourself.

Thank you to all the people I have met in my life! You matter!!

CONTENTS...Page

Alcohol.

You can use it with ice to make it cool down,
You can flavour it up as one swills it around,
You can sip it in quiet so not to make much noise,
Returning to childhood, you're not playing with toys.

Drink it at home, from the world it's a wrench,
Slurp it in the park where life's home is the bench.
Some do it for politeness or a thing they've not tried,
I myself in honesty for the effect once inside.

The clock it keeps on ticking, don't realize it's begun,
The voice it keeps on saying, "yes just another one".
Suddenly without warning, your senses begin to slow,
You by now realize what the other people know.

Fix your grin even wider, stiffen the body into a groove,
No matter how you try to look, the room, begins, to move.
It is about this time, depending on how much you've had,
That your soul can be made happy, perversely quite sad.

The reaction of the people around you, can be a choice of two
just the same,
They set you up for benefit of humour, or turn away with
disgust and disdain.
Where do all your friends go when you end up on the floor?
Gone, departed, ended, as they found you just a bore.

Lonely, lost, disjointed, there is a fever in your mind,
Wet, pissed up, unsightly, why is it you remain so blind?
Finally, when it's at it's most potent, you're there with jelly like airs,
The mind succumbs, stops turning, your dreams now govern your cares.
©Chris Matthews.

<u>Alcohol</u>

All Night Café.

Approaching the solitary window,
Cold bites deep to my veins,
The belongings to the window's innards,
Crack out wards, light up my way.
The glowing warmth and smell of it's doorway,
Invites you, to the 'All Night Café'.

Breath lightly on the window,
Cold wind catches it hard,
One moment caught from moving,
All sense of feeling barred.
Huddled in the corner, mug of tea to hand,
Covered in rags is the resemblance of man.

He has no knowledge of his surroundings,
Which have treated him so severe,
He keeps on hiding from us nightly,
With yet one more pint of beer.

See sweat filled walls look down on solitary man,
Sits crumpled and worn, preserves what dignity he can.
Wind leathered face, stiffens disgrace.
Unshaven, unclean. Visible and smelling are the places he's
seen.

Look into his eyes, they are swollen brown,
The darkness of which match only his frown.
His cheekbones in contrast, stand out proud,
Skin, clinging thinly, as his corpses constant shroud.

Decide to move in closer, having been unnoticed inside,
The staff sit living in the kitchen, where from such reality they hide.
Still, he sits coldly, as I, invading his space,
My form forever lowering, stops, opposite expressionless face.

For a moment my attention is taken, by a voice high ticking on the wall,
It's face forever changing, one day it too must fall.
Outside howling, the wind is crying to get in,
Starts kicking at the doorway, raising the noise to a din.

There is laughter in the back now, as the clock it strikes one,
Everyone seems to be saying, "life must go on".
Turn back to the table, my friend has a tear in his eye,
All the lonely people in the world, yet nobody answers why.
Reach out to touch him, then all I wipe is on glass,
His reflection my visage, these moments would not last.
©Chris Matthews.

At The Bridge Tonight.(Song)

Am
I hope you come down to the Bridge tonight...
Am7(5th fret)
Bring the guitar you know it's right...
Am
At the Bridge tonight....

Many a person comes and goes...
What do they seek? Nobody knows......
At the Bridge tonight...

Enter the door you'll feel at home...
Plenty of space for your head to roam...
At the Bridge tonight....

Pull up a chair 'N' take a seat...
Lend your ear to a steady beat...
At the Bridge tonight....

Pour me a glass, one or two...
It's a love of life to share with you....
At the Bridge tonight....

Smiles all round, beautiful thing...
Feel the groove get in the swing...
At the Bridge tonight....

Too many to mention who play along...
So join on in and sing this song...
At the Bridge tonight....

Hurtles to midnight, going strong...
Move with the group's heavy throng....
At the Bridge tonight....

Time soon goes when you're with friends...
But the music and laughter never ends...
At the Bridge tonight....

Last moment for a final refrain...
An echo is all that'll remain...
At the Bridge tonight....
©Chris Matthews.2015

Blind. (Song. Capo on 2nd)

```
E                                      A
```
Look outside my third floor flat window, didn't know what I'd
find...
Try and search for something exciting, it's driving me out of
my mind...
Have another drink from the cup on my sink that's the way to
get by...
Take another drag on my electronic fag and I'll die...

```
D                              A      E
```
Whatever you do, hold on to what's true so be kind...
There's a knock at the door, I think it's the law, so I'm blind...

Go outside I stand in my shadow, it's a hell of a way to live...
Followed by invisible forces, just who's the captive....
Get a job sweeping up roses, from the lovers who've split....
Stand around waiting on tables, no one here so fag lit..

Whatever you do, hold on to what's true so be kind...
There's a knock at the door, I think it's the law, so I'm blind...

Mobile phone rings it's the girl who through things in the
dark...
Flowers were thrown at the boyfriend alone in the park...
People walk on the petal strewn ground don't stare...
She walks past a crowd of people who simply don't care...

Whatever you do, hold on to what's true so be kind...
There's a knock at the door, I think it's the law, so I'm blind...

I speak in a tone that makes me feel prone to her voice...
My senses pick up when she speaks and offers a choice...
My place or hers the thought sends me into a dream...
Reality strikes when I realize I just want to scream...

Whatever you do, hold on to what's true so be kind...
There's a knock at the door, I think it's the law, so I'm blind...

Decide not to go time now goes too slow I flop down...
King for a night as dreams take my fight drop my crown...
Eyes start to close on the girl with the rose I'm alone...
No light to see as sleep seizes me now I'm blown

Whatever you do, hold on to what's true so be kind...
There's a knock at the door, I think it's the law, so I'm blind...

©Chris Matthews.13/01/2015

<u>Christmas.</u>

Christmas.

Children sing now 'Silent Night',
Huddled beneath their bed sheets tight.
Remember all that's past this year,
Imaginary Santa's in dreams appear.

Soon to come an infants birth,
Remember mothers this time of mirth.
May their wishes all come true,
Amid this festive retinue.

Share goodwill and Christmas cheer,
Save those close you feel dear.

Christmas comes but once a year,
Hold a thought for those not here.
Relish now what you've got,
Impart some time for those who've not.

Simple things as presents give,
Take not for granted, this life we live.
Make new friends, take old ones back,
Amoral is the gold we stack.

Share good will and Christmas cheer,
Send this now to all who hear.

Come one and all it's Christmas time,
Hear joyful song, my love is thine.
Revel now in God's neat sight,
Immerse yourself in his sweet light.

Sing with others far and wide,
The joy of season, this Yule tide.
Merriment with all abound,
As carollers take their songs around.

Share goodwill and Christmas cheer,
So all salute, yet one more year.

Best Wishes, ©Chris Matthews 2012

<u>Communication</u>.

Communication.

Communication of old; was using mirrors or Smoke,
Now we speak on phones, keep chatting till we Choke.
Text away, to hearts Delight,
Even corrects, when we're not Right.

Landline. Radio. Mobile or Skype,
Type.. is now consigned to Landfill,
Downhill.. into History,
Mystery.. of signals.. lost in Space,
The advancement of, the human Race.

Have you ever phoned a help desk and been put on Hold?
Sold.. the notion, your call is Salient,
Ambient.. music to soothe your Ears,
Fears.. of abandonment hurt your Pride,
Disillusioned when; you find they've Lied.

Sometimes a robotic; voice is on Call,
Fall.. into the trap of an automated System,
Listen.. to the monotony of inputting Numbers,
Slumbers.. the mind, into a somnolent Dream,
Beauty.. to be woken, by a prince's Scream!

All we want, are human Voices,
Choices..Given; Not taken Away,
Dismay.. when faced with tunnelled Menu's
Venues.. arrived at, by corralling the User,
Communication is the only Looser.

Please be aware this call maybe Recorded,
Just as the system and government Ordered.
Careful what you Say and Do!
Someone.. may; Eavesdrop on You!!

Crossroads.

Waiting at the crossroads for the daemon to arrive,
Strive for perfection, playing guitar,
One day I'll be that blues playing star.

Many a soul has trod this road,
Strode to the one to make their pact,
Make up for things their life has lacked.

Thirst a plenty, the minds a rush,
Hush the fear as night closes in,
There's more in this world, I'd call sin.

What of others alone at home?
Roam their minds while they're asleep,
Trust in God for them to keep.

He hands the paper like the dole,
Stroll in the park, for one who's caged,
Uneasy choice for all unwaged.

Signed in blood like an old pay slip,
Rip against a system, thats all we do,
Few and far the choices, given to you.

I volunteered my soul for a better life,
Strife is an illusion, what is there to gain?
I am lonely once more, left with my pain.

Go to my children asleep in bed,
Bled from their future, have I done wrong?
The truth is: I just want to belong.

So when you pass me playing the blues,
Muse over where, You'll be one day,
Keep the demons in Gov. at bay.

©Chris Matthews.2014

End of Work. (A Villanelle)

I look towards the heavens and a water droplet hits my hand;
Stare straight up, now falls a seed in my eye.
I take it and plant it on the land.

My feet clomp through, on clotted earth we stand,
Reach the field boundary then sigh.
I look towards the heavens and a water droplet hits my hand.

Storm prowls across with an urgent demand,
Fear presents itself to me, stand idly by:
I take it and plant it on the land.

Dark forces, more than we understand,
Conjure up imagery from on high:
I look towards the heavens and a water droplet hits my hand.

'Animal Farm', is not fairyland!
The 'Spiders from Mars' are not a lie!
I take it and plant it on the land.

With our moisture sucked away, leaving nothing but sand,
We toil on till we die,
I look towards the heavens and a water droplet hits my hand,
I take it and plant it on the land.
©Chris Matthews.03/04/2014

Finally.

To sleep, to dream; through the turmoil of the night,
The one wish of the non-sleeper; is that you?
So still, so rare, imagined image takes flight,
Somnolent thoughts of fear and hope now ring true.

I saw you in my dream and you were awake,
YOU, yearning after the ease with which I'd died.
Continue illusion long after my wake,
The rain on your face are the tears that I've cried.

You need not envy the dreams I now see,
With thoughts caught in a whirlwind without time.
Your hand on mine, the last feeling shown me,
Insomniac clock; now So sublime.
Lay me in a garden at the land of my birth,
Plant me as though I were a tree...
Then my memory will live on forever,
And my spirit will finally be free.

©Chris Matthews.09/06/15

"Goodbye, I love you".

Do you remember the last time you saw my face?
The last memory in your mind?
Take that with you, where e'er you go,
And let that thought be kind.

Did you touch my hand? Kiss my cheek?
The last time you were there?
Don't let that moment caught in time,
Be the hardest one to bare.

"Parting is such sweet sorrow",
Is what Shakespeare once said.
So say those words, next time you see,
Me drift inside your head.

Believe in God or a Higher Power,
Is what I came to believe.
Trust in this, don't live your life,
Caught in the webs we weave.
"Goodbye, I love you", is what I'd
Like to hear you say.
I'm content that you release me,
And send me on my way.

"Goodbye I love you".

©Chris Matthews.

Homeless.

There she was, picking up papers, the news everyone had read.
Stumbling now; never at ease, trying to make space for her
bed.
Rain smears down, a shop fronts' pane, raining tears down onto
her face.
How changed now, her childhood dreams, far away from this
lonesome place.
Spiteful night, hovers above, her cardboard tenement home,
Clouded eyes now look around, in this world she's all alone.
Rats and fleas, curious pests, will guard her throughout the
night.
Passers-by will look away, unconcerned at such a sight.

Wrapped in the words, picked up in the day,
Ignorant to know what they may say.
She sleeps a little, but not for long,
Too troubled by a life, all gone wrong.
Where is the family in her hour of need?
As now for strangers the hand stretches to plead.
"Out of work? Get a job"! Is all they may say,
Tragic actor? Not content! Life's not a play!!
This could happen to you or me,
I know blind men who can also see.
So perhaps the next 'Big Issue'; You will buy,
Could help end her problem and may soothe her cry.

©Chris Matthews.

If only "Love" was a name...(Song)

(G) If only "Love" was a name...
(A) I'd say it real quick...
(G) There's no-one to blame...
(A) Just need to give me a kick...
Then we walk out in town...
I take your hand...
Never a frown...
Because you're in demand...

Lean on me...
Always be my friend...
Lean on me...
I will you defend...
Like no other...
Should I compare...
Like no other...
My hearts left bare...

If only "Love" was a name...
There'd be no question at all...
With you I'd remain...
Write it large on a wall...

I'd not hide what I thought...
When I called out to you...
For it's you that I'd sought...
With the word that's true...

Lean on me...
Always be my friend...
Lean on me...
I will you defend...
Like no other...
Should I compare...
Like no other...
My hearts left bare...

©Chris Matthews.02/05/16

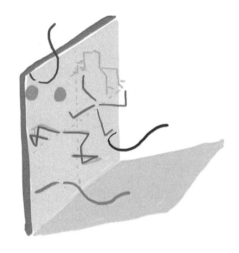

Illusion of reality.

I get up in the middle of the night, to check if you're still there,
Darkest of shadows loom back at me, as in the mirror I stare.
Everything is different through the course of the night,
Dreams go to and fro,
Everything is different through the course of the night,
This illusion of reality I know...

From my blankets caress, this shroud worn thin, I tear myself
apart.
Reach out to touch you but you are too far, the time has come
to depart.
Everything is different through the course of the night,
Cursed night shift to which I go,
Everything is different through the course of the night,
The minimum wage is too low...

Under clouded sky I set out to be at my bosses bidding,
Without the work rugs pulled from under me and down the
road I'm skidding.
Everything is different through the course of the night,
As I creep without a sound,
Everything is different through the course of the night,
Towards my duty bound...

Clinking clanking metal on metal, blast furnace heats the air,
No one alive can take the heat to arms or face left bare.
Everything is different through the course of the night,
Sparks fly fast on fire,
Everything is different through the course of the night,
Like a spirit from a funeral pyre...

Hour to hour the steel runs by, hot, raging desert's sun,
The crucible pours work into piglets and sow, fluid metal
molten.
Everything is different through the course of the night,
No sound but that of hammer,
Everything is different through the course of the night,
No chat above the clamour...

Our job done the siren wails and off home to slumber,
To sleep and dream of a days hard graft and the day I'm not just
a number.
Everything is different through the course of the night,
Put your arms around me,
Everything is different through the course of the night,
This illusion of reality.

©Chris Matthews.07/07/15

Individual.

I.. am an 'Individual', but a number marks Me!
Be it Birth, Social, Telephone, or Bank,
Thank; Big Brother for this order and Insanity,
Humanity divides me into a social Class,
Mass.. together ABCs,
Disease.. of status, will scar your World,
Hurled into the sterility of 1984,
War.. with Words not Genocide!
Hide.. the bodies in a Bag,
Tagged when they Die,
I.. am an 'Individual', but a number marks ME!

You.. are an 'Individual', and your number's written Up,
Supplied by the system, that governs by the Letter,
Better.. to choose your number, than have it forcefully Given,
Driven down to beg for Money,
Honey.. it's just our Life's,
Strife's an illusion; is what They'd have you Believe,
Relieved by the poison you have to Digest,
Invest in the people and all will be Well,
Hell.. don't be greedy and give to the Poor,
Sure.. you are needy and one thing is True,
You.. are an 'Individual', and your number's written Up!

We.. are 'Individuals', and should stand tall and Free,
See.. the benefit of labour, not filed into Lines,
Mines.. are gone and there's nothing Left,
Bereft.. of the choices our forefathers Had,
Mad.. cacophonous, politicians, argue with each Other,
Brothers and sisters are left in the Cold,

Sold out.. by bosses who've taken all they Can,
Ran away with the country, it's gone down Hill,
Will the powers that be.. just Stop and Listen,
Glisten.. the voices of the Majority,
We.. are 'Individuals' and should stand tall and Free!

©Chris Matthews.2014

(Spot the "Individual".)
23456789234567892345678923456789234567892345678923456789234
56789234567892345678923456789234567892345678923456789234567
89234567892345678923456789234567892345678923456789234567892
34567892345678923456789234567892345678923456789234567892345
67892345678923456789234567892345678923456789234567892345678
92345678923456789234567892345678923456789234567892345678923
45678923456789234567892345678923456789234567892345678923456
78923456789234567892345678923456789234567892345678923456789
23456789234567892345678923456789234567892345678923456789234
56789234567892345678923456789234567892345678923456789234567
89234567892345678923456789234567892345678923456789234567892
34567892345678923456789123456789234567892345678923456789234
56789234567892345678923456789234567892345678923456789234567
89234567892345678923456789234567892345678923456789234567892
34567892345678923456789234567892345678923456789234567892345
67892345678923456789234567892345678923456789234567892345678
92345678923456789234567892345678923456789234567892345678923
45678923456789234567892345678923456789234567892345678923456
78923456789234567892345678923456789234567892345678923456789
23456789234567892345678923456789234567892345678923456789234
56789234567892345678923456789234567892345678923456789234567
89234567892345678923456789234567892345678923456789234567892
34567892345678923456789234567892345678923456789234567892345

Job Seeker Blues.

Job Seeker Blues.

We all have, a human face,
No rat RACE!
Get a job or you'll not get paid,
Still get LAID!
Online, and job search done,
Round of applause; EVERYONE!
Unemployment's dropped, We're just a number,
Massaged figures will spoil YOUR slumber!
Government says it will pay to work,
With the minimum wage you should see THEIR smirk!
It's not the money that upsets my mind,
It's the Do's and Don'ts that REALLY grind!
Last one in, is first one out,
Made redundant, is what THEY'LL shout!
Youngsters grow, take elders job,
To the scrap heap, gently SOB!
You're not yet fifty, many years to go,
Job Seeker Blues, time goes too SLOW!
Give us a job, I'll work real hard,
Sweat and blood on my TIME card!
Keep applying but everything's gone,
'Get on your bike" was Tebbit's SONG!
Competitive spirit, whittled with time,
In the system, committed no CRIME!

©Chris Matthews.2014

Lady.(Song)

G
My Lady has flown away
Gm
Time is slow now through the day
           B (note)
It's good I wish her.

Easy now to say
We both must find a way
I sure will miss her.

C   Csus2/Bm7   A
One of these days we're going to party on in the sky...
Time to look back...Laugh but we won't cry...
G   Gm   B(note)
You might be gone but I'll not say "Goodbye..."

Let the music sound
Just like you're still around
It's good I wish her

The love I could have found
May somewhere else be bound
I sure will miss her.

One of these days we're going to party on in the sky...
Time to look back...Laugh but we won't cry...
You might be gone but I'll not say "Goodbye..."

Sweet "Adieu" remember You
With the colour never blue
It's good I wish her

Find Love in all you do
Friends always is so true
I sure will miss her

One of these days we're going to party on in the sky...
Time to look back...Laugh but we won't cry...
You might be gone but I'll not say "Goodbye..."
You might be gone but I'll not say "Goodbye..."

©Chris Matthews.28/04/16

Lost Love.

My heart bleeds an emotional torrent,
I am bereft of words and lost in thought,
As the love I wanted cannot be caught.

Where to go now?
What to do?
Knowing I'll not walk with you.

Stand tall Gardener,
Accept tears as your bird flies free,
I hope one day, you'll know what you meant to me?

My Bacchus cup overflows,
I am lost in time,
The Pierrot does his solitary mime.

It's all a dream,
Life's too short,
For this night to distort.

Finally when despair is at it's most potent,
You're numb with jelly like airs,
The mind succumbs is silent; your dreams now govern your cares.

©Chris Matthews...---...10/08/2014

Media.

The prattle of the TV's blare,
The transfixed masses stare,
24hr news makes it clear,
Don't believe what you hear!

Entwined In the words that they say,
Falsehoods designed to sway,
Who's agenda is it tonight...
To know what's wrong from right?

Headlines created, make us feel,
Too horrid! Are they real?
Where's the good in this pleasant land?
Scared to watch on demand.

Press the button to get your fix,
Children's minds will soon mix.
Start them early, see the vision,
Later leads into derision.

Parents really should blame themselves,
On what their child now dwells.
Any wonder they're all in fright?
Day's news, another fight.

Getting fatter sat on the couch,
Jump in fear, run stop crouch!
Where's the games that we used to play?
Gone are those from our day.

Electric gadgets now litter,
All our baby sitter.
So what of Art and reading books?
Dusty shelves, no-one looks!

We should take time to reassess,
Change the times, let's redress.
The power these media have on all,
Me for one does appall!

Take time to meditate,
I realise now that life...is great!
I Pull the plug and switch all off,
Media!! Now bog off!!!

©Chris Matthews.29/07/2016

Memory of a lost love.

He sat, motionless, a hard static stare.
Trapped now frozen, to a small rocking chair.
Looked out over garden, so wonderful, so wild,
Bringing back the memory of when she last smiled.

Trapped by the thoughts, steel cogs twist in his mind,
Revenge has consumed and made him so blind.
Winter blown leaves, yellow and brown, blur his vision,
Chill-Blaine memories turn to such derision.

Thoughts of auburn hair and emerald eyes,
Many nights spent, with love's low muffled cries.
No children to share, for impotent man,
The bedtime rows, the tears that ran.

She left him she said "'cause all was not fine",
For him it was, "just a matter of time".
Knowing of the others, she'd seen for the night,
No doubt his heart was too broken to fight.

Love now gone, was such a temporal game,
Some amorous nights? So who was to blame?
Tears like rain for this solitary soul,
Like a resting actor, who has no role.

Although outside, was now breezy, quite warm,
Inside his heart bled, so tattered and torn.
Clinging with care now, to what he had left,
Pictures, happy times, memories would test.

Where could he go now? He could not complain,
Sat there anguished, was her victim, inane?
Why are some people so selfish with life?
They make a bad lover, husband or wife?

A flower calls back, seems to call out loud,
Peels back the folds of his self imposed shroud.
A glimmer of hope in this field of colour,
Reflects glints of light to a face full of pallor.

The child within him, runs out now quite free,
To the arms of a waiting, old oak tree.
So wise and loving, caring and strong,
Away the memory of all that is wrong.

Climb up higher, go in search of the light,
His garden a vision, so calm and so bright.
He holds hands with his child and goes on a walk,
Path of discovery, long shall they talk.

Where ever there is Black so, so there is White,
As the end of the day, follows to night.
Keep hold his child, forever a team,
To be at one, with life now, his dream.

©Chris Matthews.

Miners (on Mandolin)

D
The pits have all gone
D
We know what went wrong
G   Em
The imports have sealed their fate.
Brother to brother
Down mine shaft and other
Now they've closed the last gate.

Chorus
D
The black gold's still there
D
Will nobody care
G   Em
What rights does the working man say?
We're all a lot older
Still look over your shoulder
Those that took it away.

What was it they did
No government bid
To save the mines from their close.
It's all too easy
When the governments "squeezy"
Sure don't smell like a rose.

Chorus
The black gold's still there
Will nobody care
What rights does the working man say?
We're all a lot older
Still look over your shoulder
Those that took it away.

Hard working man
Done the best that he can
Toil for an honest days pay.
Up to the sky
Head home now to cry
No laughter like back in the day.

Chorus
The black gold's still there
Will nobody care
What rights does the working man say?
We're all a lot older
Still look over your shoulder
Those that took it away.

©Chris Matthews.2016

Poppy Strewn Fields.

War is turmoil; over a blood red sea,

Now stand with poppies to remember me.

Lest we forget, those who've died,

Boys, the men, the nights I've cried.

Blown down, twisted; flesh from bone,

In Flanders fields, laid so prone.

When brave men went to war that day,

Waved goodbye, to their fiancé.

Little did they know, most would be caught,

By death's dark calling; this war they fought.

From trenches they marched, into the fog,

Caught up on barb-wire, trapped by the bog.

Ears bombarded as bullets fly by,

Twisted by the echoes, a friend's last sigh.

Never retreat into the sun,

One last stand, then fell by a gun.

Pictures, a letter, is dropped at our door,

This soldier never returned from his tour.

One day I'll see your poppy strewn fields,

No more wars, for guns and swords to wield.

©Chris Matthews.

Rules.

Rules. Rules! Rules!! We learn them all the Time,
Rhyme or Reason; School or Work, when broken make you
feel like Jerks,
Perks.. of the privileged; is to break them at Will,
Still..believing they're immune, to the laws of the Masses,
Classes.. of people not like You and Me,
Free.. to do nothing except Hum-bely.

Rules. Rules! Rules!! For young and for Old,
Sold.. the idea by the legal Elite,
Mistreat them at Cost,
Lost.. in translation, of legal speak and Latin,
Satin.. and ermine, fabrics they Wear,
Care.. not for the man, who on books they make Swear.

Rules. Rules! Rules!! Ten Commandments, are Enough!
Yet the laws from the system can really be Tough,
On Citizens who merely, want to get By,
But some of the rules, make me breakdown and Cry!

Rules. Rules! Rules!! We're confronted each Day,
If when speaking our minds, across a line we do Stray,
They'll clobber the dissenters merely for Fun,
 So we talk with fear, till our campaign is Won.

Rules. Rules! Rules!! They must think we're just Fools,
Tools.. for working and nothing More,
Poor.. are we in pockets; but not in Minds,
Reminds Me there's other things, important Right Now!
How.. can we bend so low to the Soil,
Toil.. for a pittance, before we Recoil?

Rules. Rules! Rules!! We use them as a Measure,
Pleasure.. is the promise that we'll be Alright.
Right up 'Shit Creek' without a Paddle!
Twaddle.. of the politicians and all of their Gang,
Bang the drums; Sound an Alarm!
You'll not get me, to shake their greasy Palm!

©Chris Matthews.2014

Sleep Little baby. (Song)

Am   E
Sing me a lullaby send me a dream....
like the child from it's mother who one day must ween....
G   Am
Safe in your arms tender and warm...
E   Am?
Stay there forever free from all harm...

Sleep little baby till morning light...
Sleep pretty child everything's right...
One day you'll grow tall as a tree...
That's when I'll know you need to be free

What will you look for, what will you seek?
Always be proud but remember the meek...
Be fair, be wise and humble to all...
I'll still be there if ever you fall...

Sleep little baby till morning light...
Sleep pretty child everything's right...
One day you'll grow tall as a tree...
That's when I'll know you need to be free

Until that day I want to hold onto time...
Though there be rivers to cross and mountains to climb...
The path maybe winding narrow and long...
I hope on your way you remember this song...

Sleep little baby till morning light...
Sleep pretty child everything's right...
One day you'll grow tall as a tree...
That's when I'll know you need to be free

©Chris Matthews and Christine Turner.13/09/15

Son.

Nine months we waited, to see who you might be,
Many a restless night worn thin.
Through adrenalin rush of the birth set free,
Waxy covered redness of skin.

Laid asleep in my arms, my prayer had come true,
You were complete and all was so good.
I promised then that I would always love you,
The way a parent always should.

Although through our lives we've not always been together,
In my heart you'll ever be.
The word "family" will always be our tether,
Your spark in life is still free.

Many a year has struck, circled round mortal clock,
Some were so warm, some went blue.
But if at my door there was a sudden knock,
I'd hope in my heart it was You!
©Chris Matthews.27/05/2015

TAX.

The bedroom tax has now arrived...
No longer needed by those who've died...
Many have left this mortal world...
Killed by taxes the government hurled.

When Henry the eighth wanted more...
He decided to go on a country tour...
Window taxes were his demand...
Throughout the land, many were damned.

Now Goods and services are taxed to the hilt...
They tell us that's how our country's built...
Those that earn more simply hide it away...
While the poor live malnourished in poverty and decay.

There used to be soup runs for those who queued in line...
Now there are food-banks, a testament to time
What of the money banks who take all our wealth?
Bailing them out was another tax of stealth!

The bonuses they take when giggling on Champagne...
Causes the people...so much more pain...
Have's and have nots are where we're at now...
Some politicians milk the given cash cow.

Expenses for those who've already too much?
Second home in London, two jags duck pond and such...
Parliamentary money has gone amiss
Well time is time...they're taking the piss!!

Four hundred a month for food with no receipt...
MPs can afford the best cuts of meat...
Sometimes they've taken figures from the air...
So much for the ones stuck on welfare.

Proper jobs are needed if we're all to live well...
Equality of people is on what we should dwell...
Where will it end; with a tax on our breath...?
One thing is true we're all taxed till our death!!

The Day I Saw You.(Song)

```
C                          Em
```
The day I saw you was the day I loved you....
```
Am                         G7?
```
The day you left was the day I cried....
There's many a word to say if you knew....
How many's the time we have tried....

With every day it's a little longer...
The time the tear falls down my face....
Never known to feel such a hunger...
Never felt so out of place....

You are the light I'll never sever....
You are the one that kept me strong....
You'll be in my heart forever....
You'll be my friend who does no wrong...


```
C                          Em
```
The day I saw you was the day I loved you....
```
Am                         G7?
```
The day you left was the day I cried....
There's many a word to say if you knew....
How many's the time we have tried....

Thought I saw you pass my window....
Where do you go all the time....
Many darkest night long shadow....
To remember you is not a crime....

So you'll stay beautiful in my mind....
You're free like a bird to fly on high....
I only hope good is what you find....
As with this song we say goodbye....

C   Em
The day I saw you was the day I loved you....
Am   G7?
The day you left was the day I cried....
There's many a word to say if you knew....
How many's the time we have tried....

©Chris Matthews.2015

The Gardener.

I walk through a garden, so wonderful and wild,
Find a place now, for my inner child?
As I try to pluck a flower, of my chosen hue,
All I hold,... are images of you.

Your face a picture, the camera my mind,
I'd see you still, even if I were blind.
Forever etched in my psyche, there is no compare,
My heart is open, my soul laid bare.

Blow on; the wind,...sower of seeds,
YOU are the gardener, shredding the weeds.
Your Winter is gone. Spring is now here,
The fruits may grow, in a field without fear!
From the soil to the growth of an old oak tree,
Roots take hold like my care for thee.
If planted and nurtured well with time,
Maybe one day, I'll have the love of thine?

Can emotion blossom, if not watered from the start?
A nod,... a glance would really be smart....
Please allow me an insight, how you might feel,
So I may know now, if this enchantment is real....
©Chris Matthews.08/08/2014

Waiting Around...(Song)

(C Maj7) Waiting around for no-one,
(B7 sus) Been waiting here for years,
(C Maj7) Waiting at the lonesome bar,
(B7 sus) Filled with all my fears.......

(G) Someone came and took my hand,
(C Maj7) Could it have been you?
(G) We danced together through the night,
(C Maj7) All my dreams came true........

(C Maj7) Waiting around for no-one,
(B7 sus) Been waiting here for years,
(C Maj7) Waiting at the lonesome bar,
(B7 sus) Filled with all my fears.......

(G) We danced until midnight,
(C Maj7) Then you ran away,
(G) Was your carriage pumpkin?
(C Maj7) I wished you could stay........

(C Maj7) Waiting around for no-one,
(B7 sus) Been waiting here for years,
(C Maj7) Waiting at the lonesome bar,
(B7 sus) Filled with all my fears.......

(G) Search the streets to find you,
(C Maj7) Seek where there is light,
(G) Cab goes by, See your face,
(C Maj7) But then you're out of sight.......

(C Maj7) Waiting around for no-one,
(B7 sus) Been waiting here for years,
(C Maj7) Waiting at the lonesome bar,
(B7 sus) Filled with all my fears.......

(G) Next night I wait there,
(C Maj7) Hope that you'll come in,
(G) An empty seat next to me,
(C Maj7) The music wearing thin.......

(C Maj7) Waiting around for someone,
(B7 sus) Been waiting here for years,
(C Maj7) Waiting at the lonesome bar,
(B7 sus) Filled with all my fears.......(Repeat...)(Fade)

<u>Wilderness is a Crowded Street.</u>

Wilderness is a Crowded Street.

Silence stings the ears of the hearer,
Cacophony of sound, unheard.
Loneliness turns to solitude,
Converse without a word.

Wilderness is a crowded street,
A passer-by nobody sees.
Togetherness now disjointed,
Run! I feel their disease.

Money is their mind set,
Full wallet yet they're poor.
A heart of gold inside me,
Theirs, an open sore!

Some own the World, yet are bankrupt,
Emotionally discharged black-holes.
Shiny shoes that point to nowhere,
Prices, still on their soles.

All the broken people,
Nobody tells me why.
Orphaned, divorced, mistaken,
I'll not lay down to die.

To roll over and just take it,
Is what they'd like us to do.
So let's all speak out, be counted,
Not be part, of the Zoo!

©Chris Matthews.2014